NEIL YOUNG
with
CRAZY HORSE

Big Time

Words and Music by
NEIL YOUNG

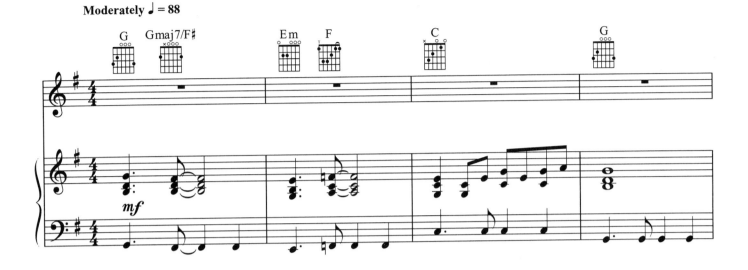

1. Gon - na leave the pain be - hind,__ gon - na leave the fools in line. Gon - na take the mag - ic
2.3. *See additional lyrics*

Big Time - 5 - 1
PF9643

4

Verse 2:
Walkin' on a bridge one day
Lookin' out across the bay,
I saw a ripplin' in the water.
Once a big ship had passed,
I borrowed a traveler's glass
And focussed on the ocean's daughter.
Kind of like a wave confused
Dancing in the sunset hues,
She waved to me and called me over.
(To Chorus:)

Verse 3:
Talkin' 'bout a friend of mine,
Talkin' 'bout a gold mine,
Richest vein in any mountain.
Talkin' 'bout the enemy
Inside of me,
Talkin' 'bout the youthful fountain.
Talkin' 'bout you and me,
Talkin' 'bout eternity,
Talkin' 'bout the big time.
(To Chorus:)

Loose Change

Words and Music by
NEIL YOUNG

Harmonica solo 2nd time

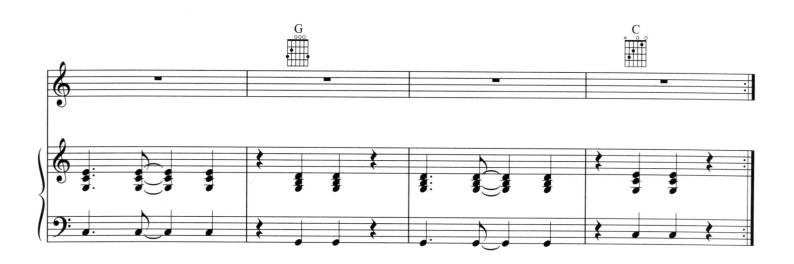

Verse:

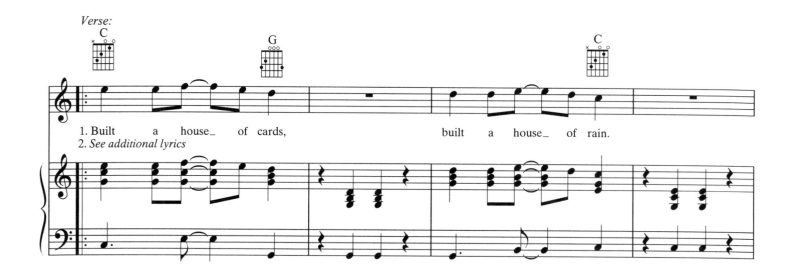

1. Built a house_ of cards, built a house_ of rain.
2. *See additional lyrics*

9

Built a house of love, build them all again.

Built a road to reason, built a road to fate.

Built a road to the Promised Land, right up to the gate.

Chorus:

Loose change in my pocket, future in my hand.

Too man-y dis-trac-tions for me to un-der-stand.___ Loose

change.___

Harmonica solo

Some roads I been fly - ing, some roads____ I crashed.__
Some roads I been run - nin', some roads I been stopped.__

To Coda

Some roads I've been__ sleep - ing__ on,___ some roads____ I got back, oh.__
Some roads I been__ walk - in'__ down,__ some roads I was lost.

Repeat as desired for solos
Last time D.S. 𝄋 *al Coda*

Guitar solo ad lib.

Coda

Repeat as desired for solos

Guitar solo ad lib.

Verse 2:
Too many distractions,
Got to get back home.
Get into something solid,
Get out of the zone.
Some roads bring renewal,
Some roads hide and wait.
Some roads promise everything,
Steal your fuel away.
(To Chorus:)

Slip Away

Words and Music by
NEIL YOUNG

Chorus:

har - bor horn___ she rec - og - nized.

And when___ the mu - sic start - ed she just slipped___ a - way,___ just like___ a riv - er roll - ing down.. And when___ the mu -

Verse 2:
High on a windy hill
The turbine did whine,
Low in the valley chill
A baby was cryin'.
Impossible to take the time,
The moment is here.
Cry out from behind the pines,
A voice coming near.
(To Chorus:)

Verse 3:
Instrumental
(To Chorus:)

Changing Highways

Words and Music by
NEIL YOUNG

1. We're chang - ing

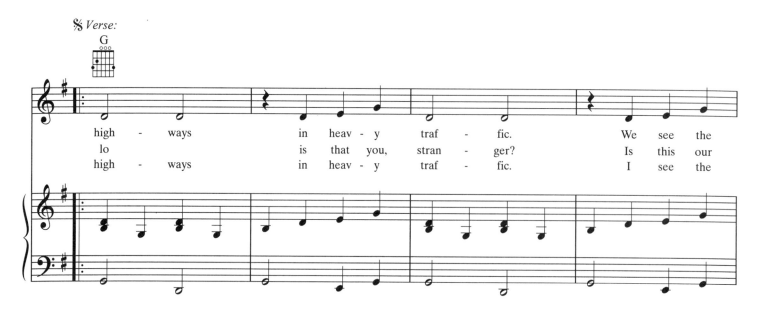

high - ways in heav - y traf - fic. We see the
lo is that you, stran - ger? Is this our
high - ways in heav - y traf - fic. I see the

Changing Highways - 4 - 1
PF9643

Scattered [Let's Think About Livin']

Words and Music by
NEIL YOUNG

lit - tle bit high, I'm a lit - tle bit low.   Hear your name wher - ev - er I go.
2. See additional lyrics

Verse 2:
I'm a little bit here, I'm a little bit there,
I'm a little bit scattered everywhere.
I'm a little bit up, I'm a little bit down.
Hear your name all over this town.
(To Chorus:)

This Town

Words and Music by
NEIL YOUNG

I'm not a-sleep when I'm ly - ing down.___ I'm a-sleep when I'm

This Town - 5 - 1
PF9643

Guitar solo ad lib.

Some peo - ple think that it's not o - kay____

Music Arcade

Words and Music by
NEIL YOUNG

Moderately ♩ = 108

Have you ev - er been

% *Chorus:*

lost? Have you ev - er been found out?

Have you ev - er felt all a - lone___ at the end of the day?___

Music Arcade - 4 - 1
PF9643

Verse 2:
Have you ever been singled out
By a hungry man?
You're listening to the radio,
He's washing your window.
When you look in those vacant eyes,
How does it harmonize
With the things that you do?
(To Chorus:)

Verse 3:
There's a comet in the sky tonight,
Makes me feel like I'm alright.
I'm moving pretty fast
For my size.
(To Coda)

Baby, What You Want Me To Do

Words and Music by
JIMMY REED

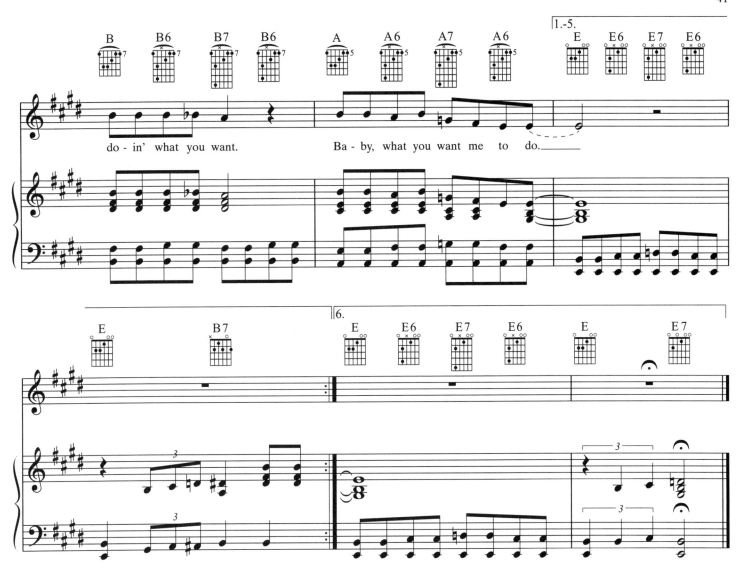

do - in' what you want. Ba - by, what you want me to do._____

Verses 3 & 4:
Guitar solo ad lib.

Verse 5:
You got me pleadin', you got me hidin'.
You got me pleadin', hidin', hidin', pleadin',
Anyway you want me to go, yeah, yeah, yeah.
You got me doin' what you want.
Baby, what you want me to do.

Verse 6:
Guitar solo ad lib.

Verse 7:
Guitar solo ad lib.

Verse 8:
You got me comin', you got me goin'.
You got me comin', goin', goin', comin',
Anyway you want me to go, yeah, yeah, yeah.
You got me doin' what you want.
Baby, what you want me to do.

Verses 9 - 12:
Guitar solo ad lib.